PRETTIER GRIT

PRETTIER GRIT

JOHN GODFREY

Station Hill Press
BARRYTOWN, NY

Published by Station Hill Press, the publishing project of the Institute for Publishing Arts, Inc., 120 Station Hill Road, Barrytown, NY 12507, New York, a not-for-profit, tax-exempt rganization [501(c)(3)].

Online catalogue: www.stationhill.org

e-mail: publishers@stationhill.org

Cover art: "BRAINARD - 71" (1971), Joe Brainard. Found box and wood scraps, twigs, clothespin, test tube stopper (2 3/8" by 3 9/16" by 5/16" deep). Collection of John Godfrey. Photographed by Elizabeth Scholnick.
Cover design: Catskill Poetic Action Network
Interior Design: Oxygen Design Group, Sherry Williams
Library of Congress Cataloging-in-Publication Data

Names: Godfrey, John
Prettier grit / John Godfrey.
Barrytown, NY : Station Hill Press, 2025. |
LCCN 2024044757 | ISBN 9781581772326 (paperback)
LCC PS3557.O29 P74 2024 | DDC 811/.54--dc23/eng/20241001
LC record available at https://lccn.loc.gov/2024044757
ISBN: 978-1-58177-232-6

Manufactured in the United States

Land Acknowledgment
In the spirit of truth and equity, it is with gratitude and humility that we acknowledge that the Institute for Publishing Arts, Inc. and Station Hill Press reside on the sacred homelands of the Munsee and Muhheaconneok people, who are the original stewards of this land. Today, due to forced removal, the community resides in Northeast Wisconsin and is known as the Stockbridge-Munsee Community.

For Alice Notley

CONTENTS

Drunk on Horizon

for Harris Schiff

Coat my eyes
          fluid skiff
     Under park canopy
          liquid forest
  Ah, the heights you claim
                    god oak
               since childhood's end
You infect me so long with
          self-guiding mottos
     inscribed on
               my Norman forehead
          To the sea, the sea

Nothing wrong with that boat
     Crew drunk on
               horizontal dream
               and me a tapwater tout
  Time wastes in sky
     I choose what I
               long for at last

     — trouble
               faster than light

Earth *Minh*

Strip of dead deep surf
            inflected with suffocation
Wary snow hawk sees bipeds
 flood black bear in light—
              meadows picnicked
into houses—
                   hills ablaze with outlaws—

Earth *minh* liberate
          earth
                with waters
             and blows
White burden tricks out so
          outsize innocent
             behind a fortune
       in fences

If you brown
                  you drown
Straight through
                      No intermission

A Million Sandals

for Myanmar

No wonder that hurt abounds in
toothpick huts, the custom of
who complains, third-world
                    whirlybird
burns through soul to spit out skin
switch from boisterous to solemn to
still unseen broken intercoms
lead paint rooms like bins
lost and found in 13E, don't jump not yet

Your skin deserts demographs and
numbness maths
your lips and tongue lose sparkle
You sit in occupied seats, you favor
electric-red open weave tunics, you let
loose local minnows in potluck sink
energy grinds out so the camera burns
bright at resentful hand gestures
two-month lease on facial misdemeanors
vendor relents for this special bullet in pagoda

Monk hollers louder than priest
Thurifer many languages before Creon

Seven-letter names for thieves and democides
ferried down watery blood
river to paddy to gulf
calendar of moons freezes its gears
Noisy walk a million sandals and
for the lucky a muted sacrifice
remarkably embalmed

Away Anytime

I love stairs
stars at the top
I love steerage for the woman
who sings there on the hour
I love stains on expensive slacks
worn by careless women
Eleven mirrors hang there
among framed oils
Perception duplicates
a painted face in lowbrow Revlon
I am dying off
as fast as my friends
The rumor outlivelies the dream
It has a horizon
docks nearby
and runaways
The dream outlives
incredulity
Innuendo though
can take me away anytime
It does not reap grimly
It stops to relieve itself
and comes back
with moist lips
a smile

Scofflaw SCOTUS

Scofflaw SCOTUS
cuts the ribbon
at the crime scene
hangs Jane Roe out back
to cure
drained
smoked

No grave!
Might rally
the unrighteous
Their Honors take the privacy
outta your pipe
and smoke it
naked under robes
in their formal chambers –
are there six or nine sinks?
six or nine sleeves
to clerks' shirts?
six or nine ball
in the coroner pocket?

Written dissent got no b.o.
needs some stinkback
Narrow reading smells
of skin bleach
and stink-ass
Close that Bible and see
will the bastards
swear on it

Light wavers
when the high bench burns
Right hand says the left hand
holds a wild card
and wilderness is zackly
where we wander

Juicy Fruit

How many the numbers run, how long the odds noir

on film, the comprehensible badness, two-three

screens on the data-fed base, permanent numeration

tag, a vessel of wits crossing the bridge, feet

wet you bet from teardrop tattoos, neighbors

neighbors, where you gone?

                                        substitute urbans miss

lawn order, plastic play-dough in accordion

purses, disparity's eggshell, the poor now fewish purged

foreign by stroke of NYCHA, this way to Division Street

both sides calibrated frosty smiles, courtesy

cling wrapped, what's wrong with that elder's wheelie

rucksack starch load, A1c huh? you can tell by

juicy fruit breath behind the mask

                                                  what's wrong with a

rifled slug in rainy gutter, busted hottle in gun hand

call wet trees sparsely feathered, call a rat a rat

in niche where two buildings never touch

Uncovered Light

Moniker don't matter for some blocks yet
Swing along your feets' path
                    but don't march
            don't buy so close to the porthole
Ritual coverings are turn-ons
      revelation an alienation
Every timeout rings its own bell
    so pack in a hurry
          Getaway is no disgrace
              in disgraceful socks
         Bounce a dime on the flatline
Shake and bake when
              they pull tonsils
          out of solid ground
    Happy song don't live up
          when you hear "Hit the deck!"
Where in all this wide earth
              bank my liver?

          Harbor tug repairs
                              in my ear
        Audio map pitched to free rads

Touchstone trips me
and bangles chime
Asleep by fits and miss the plod
through twelve-tone luncheonette
Single door for all twenty
prelates heads uncovered
including the fakes

Blown Sand

Just imagine last freedom never
plays first cause
next day boulder falls, birthday
in pixely years
sacrifice code names erotic viscosities thimbles
of gene soup in cortical pop-up truck stop
three fourths of one dimension domain
a hex under my
arms
everyone sees the mutant laugh
all the way to
the freedom bank, escort
uniformed, dapper
a chain of flowers dangles below his waist
rules immaterial adversaries brazen
uncovered imaginings in solitary pleasure
confinement well runs dry
in all due sentience
my mind stays put in
coital odor flashback
roll call liberty bowsprit
breasts gleaming
in murky discharge oblivion
rain like blown sand

Danja-russ To Be Hun-gary

Import Orban breath
gas exchange
to this third-rate nation
I take steps not to belong

200 mg Taliban tabs
as needed
in rotundas
that lose their marbles

I measure my own fur
I want it to furl
in a leftish draft
so I don't cross
the white paint line
Submit once and it's for always
Mars court martial
on Federal Mean Time

They steal law
in the name of
O lawdie!

De fucking *rigueur?*

I'll call you out

don't you call me in

You sots you fools

with ribbons and

armored robes

in the X-men test tube

My One Ear

Sometimes the person
I go to sleep as
arrives at a coven
It passes in
day-for-night black
So dark the dog rises
high as its star
Revenants scrum
and the beggar from noon
is light skinned and
clean around midnight
I can't call out a viper
with one bum arm
and need in my eye
A hole where the bonus
slips out of place in me
New faces I can't verify
Odors once of flesh
that no longer has scars

The literal word is *envie* not *besoin*
Happens with defunct and wretched –

I mean wrenched —
shoulder
It's indefensible
the shit that goes on around here
Explosions cover my one ear
Action gets cadavers to thaw
There is anxiety ahead
when you insert another dollar

Comes the moment I behave
in graceful rude
attitudes of neck, celluloid
and rage
Multicolor infants smile
out portholes
as the rocket lifts off
Fatigued to the point
I hit out
at the dark wall
until I find my pants

Discount Tired

Furthest thing from virtue
is its own ward heel
Transparent shoe to contain self
If you have a joke sashay
from honey spoon
to none of your beeswax
and worry a friend

Give with all your leftovers
when pandemic can't sleep
Hold up the wall next to
long-awaited loss machine
Discount tired

No wakeup baloney
Sky turns silver
Bus passes
downstairs like birdsong
Who do you keep this for?
Eyes open
sentiment and
concern do me in

Empty Swivel

Her color gets her cheated, well, cheat back
and walk into that lounge
A wall around the empty swivel chair
Over that wall the same again
I'd be the last to stay self-sufficient

and so drown like appendage, like coin
Choir sings to choir and
they sicken each other

Those who earn three-fifths of one care
Those who are sued at birth
step out front and solo as lonely women do

Night introduces sub-words, groans
and abrupt articulations
She is tired, I think, and
I show her to a resting place

Stone Still

Skyline crock-a-block silhouette
kind of mimeo
Plenty gens walk on by
but none in red stencil
When there's a hush it's
just dilute decibels
you pay duty for
Come hither
lonesome whistle blows
bells toll
Door to the core
where waxed hands
of consistency common
to this city which
is torch song to strivers
I speak from to-small-and-back
a Sunday lowbrow
of lofty doubts
My hand for instance in
white fertilizer on
opaque cataract color chart
It's light's out

candlestickin'

fire low, of

course I am in question

My paradise sequel

an honest fiction

I dictate when hand shuts off

heart's warm dark comfort

Cheated man in silent

chain store bravado

cool and stone still

Exposittion

La guerre est fini

Overcooked expression puts
some distance between
his face and sympathy

A realm of volunteer
trench glamor
and black market condoms

Exposition furthers:
willingness against
own best interests
leads to physiognomy
reflected double
on laminated windshield

Hero doesn't lament
the intimacies he wastes
His due, he thinks

Who is he at the border

if not underground star

He ages-out smackdab
in the center
where the curve
is at its lowest

Drab façade with
posh interiors
Prefers to carry
middle of the night

Solo performer on the road
Welcomed according to outdated myths
Plans the dispute within view of a cemetery
Not the one he mostly uses

Slaps Away

I buy another day
and listen all through it
A question for Fu Manchu:
Why does she move me again
why do I stir?
My fingertips throb
from one peek
at her thighs
Her laugh so like
a thought she slaps away
Memory kisses deep
and I get hard
Burnt poison her rage leaves
and I toughen
If along her street there were
another chance
I would not break its sorrow

I sleepwalk in deception
and desire
She is above me
she tumbles upward

I might never see a horizon
her breasts are so stateless
and sleep slices thin
I see blood on its way
from an orange moon
to flush her cheeks
A pricey set of sheets from Babylon
and how I care

Man-Made Bodies

Midsummer might dream
promise brakes hard
to end at ceremonial table
        with sow purse

Hardhats in gone zone
        brush newly-papered walls
Deep penetration
            and shallow flies
Nah, not her thing

A founding truth
        prior to grab-bag illusion
She means to be close
            to tautology
        where to be
doesn't fit in
        man-made
                bodies of water
She redefines the variables

        so that's what I tell them

Burned Light

Remedial burn carboniferous cluster suck
changes moon to nebulous blue
                                        rain shafts
wind instills confidence game and fourth pyramid
I come out looser well-tempered
hair roots dry sky off
                    with one hand fantasy
                                        cast about
for fissures decorate old man with service
station fleece
                    foreshorten scuzz
nick off an hour
          skanky worship in the nut hatch
by piece work
          enter pagoda yes the restaurant
take cooked books
                    clairvoyancy sticks where
you sleep last night your number is four
lamp stays on rainbow off
                         light horses at midnight
            I dip plastic key the mini-bar is high
reach for bottle of messages to reject and

stark skin-graft seduction

pan with a hot spot

eel slightly burned

light flickers up

high then silver spray

from summits crest to crest

Frozen Freeway

View of vegetation
floor to ceiling
like the window
Every few nights
lewd back-lit shadows
I was raised on countermeasures
that pull me away by my hair

I want to burn it
Flames of air that
antagonize mud hornets
and sear the coastline where
polyglot works out an accent

Handling pays for itself

Once I feel threatened
she returns my hair
I think umbrella and hold
up my cane
If someone follows
it makes a procession

Do you ever feel that alone?

Choppiness of phrasing
identifies bilingual river
No you can't choose
which shore you are born
Words read backwards
    to advance the hug
    at the turnstile

Tracks begin to hum
Be kind to the troubled
Be moved by trouble
Trouble that covers her shoulders
as she walks away
                    Insured

Cloud Cover

This tear makes it final
All the griefs are in
one of two different cliques
My indifference
is their reward
I tolerate foot traffic
of the practical and adherent
A regime gives them life
that lives less Monday mornings
The past is how they don't learn
how little they need

Perform to get
is the course
run by need
The performer is the person
I am and don't warm to
I learn who I am
to feel needless
To perform chafes to entertain
and that person is provisional
unforeseen

and as unknown as ever

Séance, please

Muster the choice
what to color grass walls
Affectionate elbow to ribs
of the best at talking native
in breath cloud cover
A tiger of Bengal breath
cured by flexion of
cables and bones

First the place and its name
come back to me
then the face
as I shave to
an African bush song CD
This takes time
which is all mine
day for night

Hours for Cinders

My eyes pick the lock
What good's that do?
The door is warped
it makes a mushy
moss-juice sound
like I hear from night birds
among the goners
Ah, what I love ends
the whole nothing trip

Sensitive to fever vibrations
of dry thunder
Stick-pants weather's
vault of tumbled cloud
Confession:
This is your body
at work on my silt
Footprint mud *frittée*
at Cone 4
Light match
to thc correct kiln
It takes hours
for cinders
to fall off my bones

Tired They Sleep

First-time settlers
the long walk
to East Houston
kin in the Riis
kin in the Wald

They expect little
No stars maybe a single planet
maybe a blank slate

So tired they sleep through ICE raids

If one of them is empty
and craves to learn
Let's start with rising waters
and rocks in hands

A sort of honest talent
The empty can hear everything
Knowledge especially of questions

One is not here but

here is where one is found

Sadness is the proof

Milestones

Diminish reflex drawback from hot
and cold instantly sways my attention
spates of eyesight put
together acts of faith
wait to subside
tide is gray all hours save for
flecks of white froth
midnight and noon suspension
liquid life malfeasance juggles flings
through black holes beg pardon life I
think in jokes grave grave jokes
                                        mockery continues
in and out of clothes
head-shaking rumbles under street
highway of bridges
glow fills old surrendered fortress
its straight hard-sided milestones
towering vase surmounts
attracts the reds of light
polluted and starless
stolen from newborns
full cup by cup

Available Light

Towel just won't sample my sweat
Tug on the short coat of confession

You could have left me be
beside the jukebox I
can see from
bug zappers
in outer boroughs
My mistakes result from
available light
bestilled by dice throw
Sometimes only a teeny ash

I can't make them pray for me
but the free ride
delivers to wide stairs
I run up them to cloudy cachets
of touch
Dig the fever
either underarm
Ten-ton feet plop down on
dismal alphabets

In poverty no word

for poverty

Dollar signs

Vital signs

Run signs altogether

Selling Kisses

It takes ecstatic caution
Access and discipline
my no-laughs buffoon
        Send body to chop-shop
      Serial number blanked by
              acid-fast unvarnished hijack
Gold melts on parlor skin from
            little insight to preferences
Cable up and down rib cage aflutter
              after perpetration
Advise against
          one-of-a-kind surveillance
Cruel nosiness makes a village?
        Ain't nobody here selling kisses?

Video priest moves on
He'll watch carnival
            watch overtime *couche*
          watch the driverless car
and he tells me what gates
              don't fit my key

Thunk and Open

Myopic people progenerate
                        and then some
Cold air from north everywhere
            reads to the blinded
          Hazel aura each headlight

            No hammer prayer
            fazes cataracts

but they ascend
             as I do
          ninety-six stairs
How much must I inquire
          of a face?
                       A face
is sometimes a sample

Eloge:
          the downswept
           the downright
           the sundowners

A group not a crowd
where the L train stops
waits for the door
to thunk and open
Violet hair hangs to
a man's shoulders
Crossed ankles at
the platform's edge
A fruit of the search
by chance is
a dangerous life

Your vowels don't sound
as local as you are
You turn at the point beyond which
and find your surroundings

All the Roundabouts

Readiness departs after
a modest reach for the sky
The situationist
grasps the microphone
Seems fine by
the obstacle course
of sunbathers

I look shallowly
into a face
where browns yellow
on-again-off-again
blue under your eyes
Everything you give me
is like stealing your seat
before it burns

The centrifuge is all yours
sparks flash
and I'm like water
under your nails
I make vapor

Depends on
false change of season
Tree fruit drips
and knowledge turns sticky
You lick it and
groom yourself
in one of your tongues
About eight thousand miles
for hire

The pastry cost me nothing
The man at the wheel is not a born server
He knows all the roundabouts
Relax and indent your knees some
It's dark already once at
the charging station
Moon cockeyed
You in trouble

Prettier Grit

Son of light and poetry
can't finish the shot
drops the lute deep
in his own zone
So call this January fudge
after all
Strip ugly keepsakes off it

Same science assesses
maybe voice of Euridice
the wall of ears
the spilling sob
You listen, you die
in dirty fable
You rearview, she
goes bye-bye at the buzzer

Assurance strays through
prettier grit
In-flight bassoon
out of self
locks into adagio

Sleep astonishcs
        all through liberty

Wake up in ballroom
          without a partner
    Deep in earth
wise men in step-ins
       sweat alcohol
    as she follows you
  almost home

Rubber Stone

During that Chinatown encounter words
imitate thought like
wood does heat
mendicant tosses off dry
aside fleet couplet mocks
glue on principles of
non-adherence
words stick small pleasures
in tease of meaning
the other monks I
dollar here dollar there
afterworld they sleep in
'til cold stirs 'em up
I shortcut angles to a warmth
many can see
dark so fast
nubs of frost
memory pays cash order

there is no first cause
there's a Malian guitarist
like rubber stone

there's a longshot

for the loving and aloof

Hands To Wash

The idol is waiting
The idol is lavished and bathed

Her legs spread head lolls
under mushroom cap

Skin from a previous life tingles
when my desire runs deep

My mind has hands to wash
I know precisely which fetish clings

Pleasure shape-shifts
the sides of my head

Laughter engraves broken
lines on the joyride trail

Throw Rug

My heavy hand wrapped
not in carpet but
in throw rug
A touch to my nose
which inhales
with stoic imagination
the scent of her vulva
her true ephemeral
armpit smell
trimmed not waxed
Particles shower out through windows
from helical sources
no longer called lover
Hypothetical dust I don't measure
when I count time
My body holds against
the *dernier* day
One by one
the rest of them
release their virions and buds
and each mutation
lasts because I change

I forgive my choreography

for forgetting its own self

to be true of me

Will Do

I try to tell padded bluster
        from dramatic calving
Someone mutely falls apart but
      holds the biggest chunks together
She subscribes to her own fury
              Hot steel blade tempered
                in grape jelly
Use your eyes:
                        there is also
              a blackened spoon
                      in the hatchback

Reconstitution resembles
         a frottage joke
and the stenciled number
                on the rookie camel
Connect the bones as I plow
              the seas under and
        coax memory into whispers

The body selects its own piracy
                  impelled to confusion

I forget where the pleasure fits in
Can't be a dream, the clock
        is running over
            my feet of bisqued clay
I have to learn my way again
      around Disenchantmentville –
my new favorite problem
Any place will do

Whoodah Hat

Clouds merge
oily blueberry hindsides
Cup hands for
raisins of snow
in the negative
northern exposure
Woeful memory additives
The moment I should
touch her face
long enough ago
in flared pants
and infrared nose
Where is she when she wants me?
I don't do Alley Oop
maybe don't
do honest
Wooden coins flip
behind my eyes
Ten pennies a second
Honest Abe's profile blurs
into Corinthian columns
Initiation whoodah hat

bespeaks nothing of consequence

Cheap-fogey regrets

all the

long way home

Three Trains

Just above my teeth is my personal
heaven's rest where three trains stall
if you want to find me there's
a mole near a patched-over tattoo
four letters in a language some roots
some water to bridge over a five-year old's
voice from too far inside a surnatural
pitch in pentatones and loose pants
heavy footwork and hand
jive for grave accents like
the opposite not always rings true the distance
between us closes you move out of the light
something to be said a felt soft objection
it brings you air to breathe out and
you do what I would do

Denial Rhymes

You say Sherlock Holmes or Stockholm Syndrome?
preferential rhyme denial
as simple to abuse
as desire cures
need a virtual latch
for that key
sun, wave with your heat
it goes outward
like smokes go
in dream
on Saint Avenue
view changes, windows under river
clunkety-clack tunnel
bottoms out so
buffets dog it uphill
duffel spills smoked priestess
one way into and out
of clothing rudeness
for plaid word doll
denial rhymes with
preferential
new-brand loyalty
is how you know

Shaded Crown

I listen to song
finch or sparrow
I don't know which
The human factor
is not a union shop
To swim together or right to breathe

Keep to myself voluntarily
despite raw sun's play
on dark youthful skin

Parade of no panty lines
and residual intimacy
beckons to no one
No priceless sentiment
no velvet scraps

Sun takes to its couch
Pigeons wheel in
the crack-the-whip game
gracefully rowdy
brilliant white

rounding westward
Blackened gray heading east

Then back in
hierarchical accord
to the shaded crown
of a single park oak

So I Dance

I know one more trick
but it
might make you sad
The simplest trick
in several movements
and no add-ons
I only perform it
twice, in taxis
So, automotion is a plus?
You got an app?

Destination 9.7 miles

Avenue of hospitals flits by
To fly out of town
I also pass graveyards
in Queens
Ensures I stay
aloft and sober
New habit attracts negative habit
for the better
Then I am built like

body as bungalow
with crimes of passion
and termites

Sounds tropical, search for
Island Paradise, the Paramusical
First reel, fan dance
Second, beach towel dance
Third, gunshots at my feet
so I dance
Not naked, I don't know where
I might have to run
Like, naked until five minutes ago
when I don't just imagine
I *am* my mortality, and stateless

Brush Touch

Walk to the left around affair
Summon no one appropriate
Let skin settle down
after brush touch
Ears induce ringing
Blood flow excites
          boxheaded elder
I just don't know anymore

Tenderness were it elastic
               through the maildrop
Same oath as uptown
          on girlfriend's stoop
Has to do with various exes
                    and frankly
            fire goes right through
                              my nitespot

Foreigners who know
stop at white lights
Execute first
                 Conceive later

It’s in the world and
        not shy of poems
Skirts cling ‘til I’m burnt out
No actors no boards no trod
Being and nuffingness

Someone up the stoop
leans close
            Hot night decides
            the odds I meet you

Chain of Clouds

Mind impales on
chain of clouds
Tufts of hair link
taste of erotic gas
Ninety-three million
miles of light plus
ten feet through window
Shaded cleft of breast
Defined skirt of vulva
Wings scoop out my eyes
Physical flight
under X-ray sheets
Were there ever
greater pleasure
A wall tumbles and
lets out the universe

Hellbent

Naked is as naked de-liberates
flesh tones restrictive
lesson before dying, gray
bones dry over
last night's fire
Sequel in mind of nomad
land of monads
escape non-flammable searchlight
cold halogen dick
Why can't you tell she's a child
once you aim
mind the limit on granmas

I melt my hands in firefights
dunk them in ice chips
hold them up to smoke
shop lights in
the Borough of Churches
I falsely think a ribbon of blood
makes my feet stop dancing
I ring the bell without information
to add to the video

Murder just outside my heart
makes it yearn
Break of day states
the question plain:
everything's still hellbent
the swinging spider with
white dots on black
in a dream of
hairpiece harvest
Pale palms of hands
against glass hull
in death ship dream
distrust beseeching more than
gentleness and kind eyes
Sorrow so true it's unreal

The First Wheel

Envelope opens in vest pocket –
poison does it best
Cowboys gamble teeth
for liars with votes

Civilized humanity, aha
Yes, Grand Ole Opry

Weak thought slaloms
rigid brain chains
bends channels uphill
Someway somehow
on semi-desert
distinguish a corpse
The dead shall rise from
Great Meadows
and unite as strutters with balls
Superior
not so from pride
Rather they admire their own madness
Eat by its light consolidated
Perplexity steals
the first wheel

Determinate almost always
means kiting the buck
        Keep them checks
News chills me, I go wrap around
        steamed vascular vernacular
            the flash dance of words
          that's sister to its own language
            The "a" softens on coasts
                in house music canoes
I wrap up my past
and go off to speak of you
for the first time

Names As Questions

Day breaks surly
lays on counterpoint
percussive highlights
by gizmo
Sheets still fresh after three sleeps
and a dream that
Rhode Island cops
rough me up shout names
as questions
I holler back "Who is Charles Gayle?
Who is Sahib Shahab?"
They freeze I get my
collar straight and roll

Two own feet is all it takes
to get me raised
stick to and share
vices in the name of
my little self
Shadow makes a dog bay
while many kinds of men
lose face

perish in Epicurean analog
Don't even pretend
it's mysterious
It's an equation of light
with a dark dark quotient

What to give credence to:
the negligible in abundance
the dander of insects
the dull gold of intimacy
and incredible death

From a Flaw

Insight in wilderness
severance package
Material clues extend
beyond reach of pilots
be it candied snails
or olive lips
Deliria mutual
chez phantasme
is not just another
converted brewery, empties survive

I ask you to and you do
anoint lack in curlicues
Time after time
sidewalk torch
sputters out
Who don't know
a weakness from
a flaw?
Errancy traced down from
my totem shadow
sun delivers with

caveat durability

Could fill a hall with mess

but still there's

a wrong way home

Open trunk on

your own dime

The what brakelights mantra

The what kind of kiss is that

Fire Screen

Recall is in the present
I never say I'm not there
Everybody knows we
run aground
Three-ply footprint
and alphabet map
Then I throw my arms around

Secure and footloose, return
The roost is a humid
tunnel of pebbles
I can tell modifications
from modeled-by-time
and it's time I already served

She who sings is a bird
of a woman
My dove is aged by bugs
Distressed feathers fall back
in places, sky limit, flat roofs

Ultra-thin high stratus clouds
a fire screen to sun's bed-down
Creamsicle orange shares
on dove breast
When ruination was new I
sought more culture
The culture of trees

Eye Terrain

The woman I dream
submits to spirit
and pays twice
She thirsts for
words in sight
Arranges them
to modulate a vastness
Her eyes both
look into and out

Mahogany iris in
study of another's
eye terrain
Senses the bones necessary
to implications
Jives behind a warm
superior smile
The woman I dream dreams

The subject is "haze"
The predicate is "clue"
A little

eyeliner don't change
deep brown into tan eyes

Only under streetlights
are there shadows
between her fingers
Her slip is basic midnight
Nothing torn or stretched
Minimalist svelte
and sheltered by this hour
Her own key

Gray Wines

All my feathered guardians –
draw close
I'm talking to you, yo
move your freaky haloes
up around me
as gray wines
make me blind
You know how much
you want me to choose
blue eyes not
the brown that I follow after
follow with all of me
down the promiscuous aisles
of morning
in credible numbers
Influential color
and deadly style
I leave a quiet measure
in my thanksgiving song
to take your name in vain

As Afterlife

With what hope to search
for my soul in
even this body
A time of dyspatriation
Talk-talk slime
in the ablative
In this broken home
rigor is there
once daylight's over
I put on both gloves
to grab myself back
Intimate gridlock
among dying friends

Men up and influence women
and the women die
Like a green card waits
as afterlife
I'm bereft to remember
my youth alight
with phrasing off the beat
with lines that obliquely

lance through
coherent clouds
in polyphonic colors
Bodies that inspire
It's too much to ask me
to spare you the memory

Food and Shelter

No telling how willful is
intelligent desire
Scraps of breath between lives
despite what is fragile
The mamzelle who
stands in my soup
I use the underside of my tongue

The illusion is
the sky gets brighter
A grave bobs in the river
to drink to
Hands wait for strange skin

Like real time blows
it out of context
Description must end
to make a *modelle* of her

Lady, please, no animal
Let's keep it cologne, okay?
Umbrellas over rockpile

and half a face

on the stoop in Brooklyn

Minimum-wage-date food

and shelter stretch marks

Plus entertainment jones

Believe that come Thursday

Unequal Subjects

Flings herself over it
The barrier stands high
She lands upright

Reef in the sky shines down
on supernumeraries
who are unequal subjects

Constellations study their bets
Turn of mind feeds at traps

Your authority extends six feet
All day long it doesn't pertain

Hand touches where it hasn't since
mystery became memory

I forget you are so briefly near
Next passerby looks here, then there

Compass

Needle jabs compass
North cool for now
Waiting panders to
instincts on wings
No countdown
Tickets please
Punch blanket
of cloud
Do you smell it yet
New to the touch

Repartee ragout
Distance closes
Syllables
form the breast
I shape the volume
with hands
Fish sauce breath
mellow when hot

Skirt for rabbit F
Shirt for rabbit M

and beginnings loft

eye to eye

question to suggestion

Fingers braid

my own idea

A story of need

Needless to imagine

need plays tricks

Who am I to shun

sweet sinister things

Night Ways

Falsify a bit
to improve understanding
Lose a pawn so I can
safeguard impossibility
No soliciting they say
at the new castle
I gig there tonight on windsock
I pick pockets of air in short boxy skirts

Speaking through chainlink
I live more silent
The statuesque hostage
via parachute
calls me to a meatless meal
One of many sees the sun come up
I pray it down

Call crystal bright sky
"Gloria"
a tropic isle of photons
Embrace in an underpass limousine
Night ways continue
blinded and warm

You've had enough and you walk

Mandate that I watch

A glamorous mind

assets your frame

From behind, your hair

curtains your face

and that's

forever

Groundswell

I reach the point where
lousy is better than groundswell
Extrapolation uncinches
and slops in unusual directions
Capture it before it
evaporates or calcifies
Stay informed of
the water-cooler buzz
and the megas surrender
I enter and receive a courtesy
jacket
shirt and tie

Also
a bathing thong
and beach towel
with hula motif
I follow the eucalyptuses
blazed with seeping wounds
to Break Neck Beach
at my own risk

An idea is not
a place of
invisible ammunition
The originals are not slingshots
Girls, like arrows
cross alley valleys
You bleed from your trigger
Leather upholstery over
repurposed fencing
Plangent notes
that chill tunes
from the sin bin
The place starts to think me over

When I get there it's like
I interrupt a tête-à-tête
She folds her legs
atop the surfer bench
Whiplash tide a smile away

I see that far through glass smoke

Neon Puddles

Should heaven give
        more than it gets
    so clouds of granite
  pull me up by my wrists

Gusts shear   outside and away
    Sun lowers like
        brick-mounted zircon
    for the hopeless instead of dough

It's all mulled gravy now
Unlimited has-been
Dark roots stand
          out proud
So much no more
            (the dead)

But the older young
shake the shake

and hose drips wet
on long short-waisted legs

Face not averted
just faraway eyes
                    far behind
Passion assembles void
Broken neon puddles
reflect maroon nails
of the smallest hand
in curb-to-curb rain

Seen once making tracks
I stand at ease
          and then at rest

Lower Lip

Lower lip catches light
Her voice takes over
Power to offend is nothing but
what the injudicious want
Call it a synthesizer for eight
singers on two sidewalks
and four different stages
One vogues out in Dogon-
print suit, bell of megaphone
on right hip, mouth
and airways dark pink
compressed breath
If you record it you'll
have to do it twice
That's when your baby worries

Daybreak horizon at sea
Not like that here
Fiery start-up behind 547 East
Flat roof penumbra
It fans out as it rises
By now a woman
dresses, open window ablaze

Traffic in Air

Memory buds and a river blossoms
Dark wine still green
sails without stain of age
between brick outer walls

Pristine the voluble one
her best drunk song
under feathers and down

She doesn't chatter like
wordy finch kin
on branches
Purpose drives her to find
naked minced calories in ferment

She swallows her words
even ones a skywriter writes
edible words
shaped by traffic
in air she's
next to breathe

Partial Blackmail

Sapience has its way with milestones
Nervous peace develops

First tell my beads
then unstring them
Disable reason approximately
Indemnify the city wicket
and run against time
in the 99th Pct.
Who are you to me?

Sun boils a billion times over
Sky gutters between
brick walls and grounds itself
I breathe my own exhalations
and solitude odor
Stink of burnt fish
blown out the gills
of a bigger fish
I feel the collapse from
across the earth

Hand raises to request
memory hygiene
Can't be nonetheless
more than I am

Partial blackmail I'm talking about
Forth-and-back stroke
nostalgia for importance
To look at her and feel joy
when affect is in B minor
Cracks become mere puckers
and then smoothly seal
behind the eighth wall
and her lost name comes back

Drum Rolled in Raw

In memory of Jim Brodey

All the trappings
Beyond-pale bar glow
Lower the lights   Lower, ah yes
Alone in pilot episode times over
Highlights on clear glass
on deep polished wood
on sexy slip-ons
not meant for walking
Tips on the bar
like cabbage trimmings
at the distance she sees them from
Short dress fitting to form
Compressed hips
Knuckly knees

All unholy expectations
could be the next down dim sidewalk
Between arcing corner lamps
street allows
and keeps in check

I wonder I wonder
if courage alone as statement
makes her dick more central
Faint shadow upper lip and chin
like regretted tattoos
What sets her apart from himself
to transgress an unwanted given
Thus sits a beauty
in several lights
that determine nothing
against her will
Her power comes naturally normal
an engraved card you can identify
I can't say I'm at a loss
Clues show up for reconfiguration
and I smoke out front
Drum rolled in Raw
constant relighting
Low on matches

Dream Scramble

Middling din of rain
Shamus with
hands-free umbrella

Aye, a troubling sight   pale pale door
Mind draws blanks so as
not to decline
the immediate

What I think I think
when I say scatter

Dubs-in wildlife seduction

Honor your suspicions
Crime in a dream
scramble
Getaway inconclusive

Cut to yellow cab
Through windshield --
impassive frown

Five Deep

Imitate a bit of every animal
Iron half the bugs out
There's so little home to shore up
and the franchise doesn't retrieve
It requires evidence and finks
Whichever way you turn
over, it's always at night

One of you's the punching bag, all
in fun, the laughter is a team song
that lacks an opponent
So love's without bouts and
it's too dark for boots

Violation promotes exclusion of
the free, more translucent than cologne
The portion who speak
try not to belong
You can't cross on foot –
hours and hours of cave

I am not the absence of you

You line up five deep, edge of the butte
The waste you leave impatiently
Those others who save you wait
in transparent cars down below

Symphony Rinse

I outlast the fixative
and stir alive
There's a soft-shoulder movie
and a bed of road
There's a strong slim neck
under wide-brim straw
I want her to top
my last difficult thought
to savor flat-taste wine
inherit three-card
sommelier in the cave

I'm off the hookah again
tapping tutti-frutti
from stone

Time, the body's grandma
of Swiss movements
Her celestial belt of nachos
gleams like milk
Semen descends and
polluted light dries grool

I imagine dark to be
true elsewhere
Floods of it close to my roof
drive me leery

To imagine tastes tasks and tuckers
Hats on all four winds
The horse with wings
a mobile has-to-have-been
She cares so much in asides
then whoosh!
She bakes Alaska
and sautés my shoes
Caramel on my fingers
bruise on my tongue

Chorus:
Symphony rinse in the hammock
You hafta wait many days to jam
mighty industries and solve sphinxes
And besides, I'm tired of your stupid white ass!

Turf Thing

Post-asphyx patois
a turf thing
Clothing articles
of instruction
What's a vintage desire
on a bias
from credible to 'solutely not
Blood moon orange peel
There is a twist, you see

I'm between distant
and hesitant
south of courage
In my sleep I cup your face
I imagine whom I might
A not-you

Streaky hawk wind imposition
Hat no magic powers
I can see to where
sight is lost
Craziest things restore it –

side-flying pigeon—

plaid with patty-size buttons—

as opposed to

my fundamental shoes

Myco-Form Balloon

Sun down-lows

luminescent myco-form

cloud balloon on horizon

Gunmetal brick wall

Solar gold square

at crease of roof

Hot I am

with surface tension

in body meme

When it comes to water

hazard how

can I miss?

When it comes to

fire I go

blind hypnosis

I crawl ahead of my skin

Whizz by as they might

wings do not share their spread
Mushroom cloud now lavender/peach
breaks in two

Not half and half
Not in the sky we owe to

Ticket Hand

River can't save its veneer
Safe combination, yes
but not the key
Heartbeat a minute
Ask again and see
what kind of wealth
Harlequin has her price she
appears from out of a German joke
no laughing matter

Twenty years later
you remember it
as outgrown zero
hard number
has no turn signal
Cold honed steel on next truck
and you under streetlights
ride, your brights on

Slick hand slips lament
in my pillow case
REM video in unruly newsroom

and untidier subway frottage
Wine stain no matter in dream
City-bound ticket hand
Platform
revenants with a beat
Instead of sardine hors-d'oeurves
there are finger-food bubbles and
obsession jewels
Gild my phantasm
for broadcast tomorrow
when I wear Milky Way
two-inch tie
Jostle through clouds
of women in blue
and gray patterned
skirt suits
Every last one wears a cloche
Train goes on the air
airhorn first I find a
window seat sit down
drum on my thighs like no one else

Orphan Gun

Who knows how?
Anticipatory disappointment
turns tricks too close
to the surface

Nearby red oak and
spared hostage in knots
Boosters turn the
bathyscope on
and there it is
          granny's orphan gun

Up early, next question:
Steady the pins?
Worms withdraw behind me
Pursuit of share-sies ends in
real-estate poker
Wanting or wanting not
Abide

Trouble Can Float

Constructive evolution
slips a few steps back
to orbit death throe

Necessity needs to
take a chance

Magnetic like-pole
repels me from
fatuous sign-off
trade show

They touch and
touch, the twins dream
and the brazen tall
unequal guy
in bare face
breathes up the air
that's in the dream

Plastic trash snags
on the plethora of crowns
all over
          consequence

Trouble can float
much more than
you weigh

Which is metric tons
to an oyster mushroom
scarfing landfill forever
once we’re gone

Baby Blue Creepers

Sun beds down
day of the algae
Hours waste a craze of vanities
Compost in fog
feels more
rhumba than
room to let
and the devil arrives
without a satchel
I wouldn't know goodness if
I saw it in
bald tire piles
Would that mercy demand no
more than compassion
I cross the floating bridge
on fish feet
a different planet where
gold turns baby blue
Shoreline strangles lowlands
Every mirror reflects the tornado
Flattened complaint box
brain lays waste

Creepers tear off walls
ferment in bottles
until they flame

Question in a waffle cone
scooped by hand
Come on, any question, out
of endogenous fret
Shoot from the throat
I breathe through cords
to create entanglements
Unsay nothing and
televise echo chamber
Don't you *not* take the mic
Shorted-out volts
in the holding hand
for rescue at sea

Oranges and Reds

10:37 of a Friday morning
seems more grounded among
barren oak gingko
black cherry and ash
Research papers-over the tariff:
One limb a pantleg seals off
in pantyhose
Transfusion juice
on tap at
the winter picnic

Fire and coals light
the pages all
oranges and reds
in which mother learns anatomy
Skinned-away muscles
like woven petals
Half man half woman
No aspect without danger
then peace beyond expression
you don't live to see cuz
it's not there that way

Pagan Cutlet

White flight banks
its climb
on contractions
pillow all rank
hot rush like in elevator has-been
sick mouth hum
rip totem
into mini fetishes
all tastes in slumber mart
mean placesetting call it foyer-phasia
in the pokie
face paint by numbers
dress for bowleg wind tunnel
ash of root-esque starch
in Spanish mass
where do I stand on this pagan cutlet
die of the cause I am
rolled waves denude lighted beach
foundation melts
onto piss alley
gas tears woogie
courtesy of
think on it
who

Between Lips

I imagine what life
ceases to be
imagined
Undrooled kiss
on pebbly teat

Accordion musk
between lips
tonguing hair's
atmospheric moon

Swallowing gusto off
nether palate

O pasty adoration thrill
goes through me
like it's victorious

Conditions I live in know
my virtual eye

Heaven gathers skyline
as hotel room wall

Egg yolk ball behind clouds
    so bright we can see

Canary Count

Seasonal poultice and stone
Robin attacks her note
Next the pink tissue
sails on updraft
Everything sounds right
without comprehension
relief
or excitement
Dumb navigation is all of genius

Displacement sinks in
in busted shoes
on rugged terrain
Struggle to stay
on top of it
Spirit tumbles through
gravity's outlaw
Red dirt turns to rock

The glow of grease
on the ladder
turns airplanes away

Uninhabitude is my word
Canary count please
in the mine
Fumes explode from carcasses
Discarded luggage lines the shaft

I leave moss and nettle tea
in clouded Tupperware
to wet dress
a local injury
Crosshairs on a crowd
Poison tops the charts

Auctioneer points to moldy bread
In flattened furrows
bushels of gas

Left Feet

Pasture never grows back
under sidewalk shoes
cry, book bound in green
Immaculate's bell
rings lunch
at every turn limp lips
faux disenthrall
don't much matter one of each and porridge
put down the gun
take a stab at it
it sullies the skin's containment
boots to run in you associate
with navy-blue sedan red interior
in guise of the heavy squad
stage lights up boards dull
spotted with tape
exit light not far this way
follow blown-up
framed black-and-whites
of your left feet
straight to your right
bullet proof glass door
lock clicks
twelve steps ahead

Up Close

The infinity of being equal
burns law from history
Makes a whole new foolscap for me
You wear your no-makeup tool
up close on the fairway
You step out for sweet fries
Come back and sell me this?

A mountain of bloody heads in Kobane?
Syrians business side of chainlink?
La Pucelle at Disney World of Dakar?

Remove your rings for the census
If it ain't digressive, it ain't happen
` Hammer on subway bench
becomes silicon in the locked-down loo

I put a brick right here
and I stake a claim

Give it a naughty handsome flag
like the patches on a
microweave *gilet jaun*

Tiny Creased Tip

Baby crawls to a stop
Valentine clues
no evidence
Black Mask on the rail
off at 3 to 1 like
misguided third party
racks the balls too loose
She bends to her aim
blouse open
she calls the 6 in her corner
You'd think the world was ending
perpetual light
above the table
Steer clear of holy and sponge it down

I hunt mélange
find conical teeth
foreships and aft
I own but not inhabit
the color of
maroon condoms
scene is cut you

tape off the open porthole
back to your floating games
never drop your hands
never lift your slang-for-dick

No, that's a dissident street
risky cheek show
infantile otherness
my mask brushes hers
tiny creased nose
tip to tip
why I sleep by homeland river
standing up

Blanket Coat

I'm not going
then the wind changes aim
Now I go
Thoughts cross walks towards me
like Halloween

There are merits to walking upright
At night I always cast
a shadow in vape shop lights
and alone is made
for this walk
I navigate in seamy nostalgia
for the lover 50 years ago
Distant woman
self-absorbed
avid and museful

Interrupted by passing
young woman
dark eyes and hair
slim
in bright gold white and red

blanket coat

Earns 100K

Shares 4K rent

Prob'ly, or might

50 years my junior

Could as well pull

that sliver out of the moon

Not wanting leads to delusion

Not getting leads to inventory

O honeysuckle rose

Only My Alibi

Death as knockoff
CK briefs
Life as blood salad
on butt sag
Keep colors inside
the lines after dark

Others come first
at the sendoff
They lick fingers clean
bump fists...
Where's the switch
to turn up the novelty?
Room becomes a patio
with outdoor shower
Use the baby as a towel
make the breadline do time

I refuse the loaded pillowcase
and walk through the closed green door
I dirty the window and pray to the sink

Ill repute reads my name
out loud off its tablet
I catch up with my ears at a run
Tone arm rumble lullaby
That's only my alibi
I'm out of there

No song without
a language for it
Spiky notes
without rote
Beside a river
or beside myself
there are angels
with open minds
To discourage them
I offer my pride

Big New Hand

Curfew applies to
unlined face
baby-smooth skull
You can't rise can't fail
The river makes you large
and the stone from not far off
your face carves
Aquatic bird where fish are few and
the rich who choose their balconies
on top the indigenous
Who's a waif now
held by a big new hand

Drive through ruin
with the top down
You have exactly two gallons
left of narcotic brake juice
Automatically you shift
in your jock
Lips on windshield
all gentian violet
Needy and dependent thoughts

Literal on the littoral and
a bit neon liberal

Belief in a grease monkey's
life of the mind
A switchman's repetitive
daylong wisdoms
For a little while
a little while

And Plague

Clean my teeth of native bodies
curses stored up
in choral hygiene

River valleys of Redman names
emprunted by my
blinded ancestors
Natives lost in cycled reprise

Caboose conclave ends in
infected decision
railroaded by
avid roundeye perps

Sickened spirits leave
first harvest
at the mouth of exile

Thin spirochetes
small pox
yellow fever
chicken pox

measles
hepatitis
typhus
and plague

ETOH

Follow the money in land
Tillable crimes
Great White
Papa thugs
britches and boots

Birth nation bloodshed
in destinal fear
intimidations

Wampanoags   Naragansetts
Munsees   Mashpees   Mahicans
Pequots   Mohawks   Ondawas

Mohegan Sun

Smoke Rings

Affection is either out of stock or out of reach
Affection is not out of stock
Therefore, affection is out of reach

I think of several risks to take
I can't imagine the course each would run
This no longer impels me further

My life in words is all over my own hands
My heart in words is allover someone else's
There is no syllogism for this

The broken heart is not a delusion
Triumph over this is an illusion
Between the two are expressive smoke rings

Suck smoke while the reed section drowns

Like More How

Light curves out of window's
squared corners
each a lamp
I like more how
dark curves in better
than trivial liaison
Dark hides incalculable
ends of the world
Each reappears
beyond count
The lesser arrange
in jalousie silhouette

Go to the nearest star
to feel the dark
Darkness takes my love
and goes close to
someone who shares
my affaisement and
sits at a Section 8 dinette
of the spiritual
Runaway switches to glue

A hole in a cloud
makes radiance
Cardinal chirps into solo
and takes weight off the dream

Stacked Rocks

I'd respect a happier ending
if ever it begins
I'd start with deep blue shoes
under a table
the wait
for Antigone
covers fire in my tripes
with her own smoke
to humble my defiance
and make it
a cracked steel pot
I can tell stories about burial
I can tell the smell of coffin clothes

Hand full of dirt
green thumb
where she is where
she used to be
She walls herself in
with an overdose
of loyalty
Mobsters behind her
play hero

Whole town swings by a thread

Species flutter through

stacked rocks

They are bad for her

They do their right-thorough thing

Face Card

in memory of plenty friends

Allies who live on
spirits not saints
no alimentation
inside soundless vacant halls
They depend on the gelding
of a prim reaper
The cost is chalked-up to
nothingness peace
Their names paint walls
long in perspective reach

Allies who without reflection or intent
raise the barometer for
change of care
Variations complementary
to their zone too far
They are not jealous
and still have nipples
insensitive ones
which is why we divide
manias come dusk

The soul doesn't improve
            it reveals to itself
        a hot kettle of gas
that recirculates broth to one side

In hand signals memories
    that already appear
    on a page
In honor of which
    I shave my face card
    and suds my business
  don clothes from the feet up
        sit down
      and feel like this

Acknowledgements

Some of these poems have appeared in *The Brooklyn Rail* (Anselm Berrigan, ed.), *Caesura* (Austin Carder, ed.), *The Cafe Review* (Steve Luttrell, ed.), *Castle Grayskull* (Micah Ballard and Garrett Caples, eds.), *Three Fold* (Chris Tysh, ed.) and *ZaZa* (David Brazil and Sarah Pritchard, eds.). My thanks to them.

About the Author

John Godfrey was born in Massena, N.Y. in 1945. He is the author of 14 collections of poetry, including *The City Keeps: Selected and New Poems 1966-2014* (Wave Books, May 2016). He received an A.B. from Princeton University in 1967, and took a B.S. in Nursing from Columbia University in 1994. He has received fellowships from the General Electric Foundation (1984), the Foundation for Contemporary Arts (2009), and the Z Foundation (2013). He retired in 2011 after 17 years as a nurse clinician in HIV/AIDS. He has lived in the East Village of Manhattan since the 1960s.